This book belongs to:

...... Derek ....

.... lucas ....

....

Christmas Stories

stories for

7 to 9

year olds

Written by Hettie Bingham, Gaby Goldsack,
Sue Nicholson, Claire Noonan,
Kath Jewitt and Moira Butterfield

Illustrated by Leighton Noyes
(Graham-Cameron Illustration)

First published by Parragon in 2007

Parragon
Queen Street House
4 Queen Street
BATH BA1 1HE, UK

ISBN 978-1-4075-0167-3
Printed in England

Christmas Stories

Stories for
7 to 9
year olds

PaRragon

Bath · New York · Singapore · Hong Kong · Cologne · Delhi · Melbourne

Contents

A Christmas Mystery

by Hettie Bingham

Charlotte sat, arms tightly crossed, in the back of the family car. Her two young brothers had been playing a game of car-spotting, but now there were fewer and fewer cars and their game had fizzled out.

"Are we there yet?" asked Jack for what seemed like the millionth time as he wriggled in his seat next to his brother Tom.

"No we are NOT!" answered Charlotte tersely, "we're in the middle of nowhere!"

"Actually," chipped in Charlotte's mum, "we are nearly there! Uncle Jim's house is just beyond the next hill."

It was worse than Charlotte had imagined, and she had been imagining

some pretty awful things since she
had been told of their impending visit.
Christmas was going to be such a bore this
year, stuck in the middle of nowheresville
with just her parents, her two annoying
brothers and boring old Uncle Jim for
company. If they really had to go away for
Christmas, why couldn't they have gone
skiing like her friend Emily's family or,
better still, fly off for some fantastic winter
sunshine on a faraway beach?

A few minutes later, the car had
turned off the road and into a narrow
country lane lined with bare branches
that seemed to form a strange, spiky
tunnel. As they drove on towards the
house, illuminated by the low winter sun,
Charlotte felt as if they were entering
another age. Just at that moment, she
realized that the signal on her phone had
gone, along with her last hopes of an

exciting Christmas.

"Great!" moaned Charlotte bitterly, as the car swung round into the driveway of an old and totally enormous house.

"Yes, isn't it? Absolutely great!" enthused Charlotte's dad, not recognizing his daughter's sarcastic tone.

The house was built of red brick and had more windows than Charlotte could count in just a glance. At the far end of the house was a tower that looked almost like a castle's turret. Ivy grew up the wall, as green as could be, and to the right of the front door was a large holly tree, laden with red berries. At least the house seemed all ready for Christmas, even if Charlotte didn't. Waiting at the door was an old man who was waving vigorously. He wore gardening boots with his trousers tucked into them and a baggy old sweater which was patched at the arm and, Charlotte couldn't help noticing, inside-out. In the hand he wasn't waving he held a large shovel. This, apparently, was Uncle Jim.

"Welcome, welcome!" beamed Uncle Jim. He strode off into the house calling back over his shoulder. "Follow me, follow me. Wonderful buttered crumpets for tea!" and then he was out of sight, leaving just his laughter ringing in the air.

"Quite a character, your Uncle Jim," chortled Charlotte's dad as he gathered the rest of the bags and prepared to follow.

Charlotte followed her parents and Uncle Jim in through the front door and into a vast hallway with several doors leading off it, as well as an old staircase. The house smelt old and musty and her footsteps echoed as she walked across the flagstone floor and into a large sitting room. The sun was on its way down now and its last rays shone through a pair of French doors that led out onto the biggest garden that Charlotte had ever seen. She watched as her father sat down on an armchair, raising a little cloud of dust that danced merrily in the sunbeams.

A fire roared in the grate and Uncle Jim knelt before it toasting crumpets in the flames. Charlotte was feeling pretty hungry and she managed a flicker of a smile as Uncle Jim buttered a hot steaming crumpet and handed it to her. She munched thoughtfully. This wasn't the Christmas she had hoped for but it might turn out to be quite interesting after all.

While the grown-ups talked and her brothers ran wild outside, Charlotte decided to explore the house. She crept back into the hallway and up the staircase which creaked with every step she took. At the top of the stairs she came to another long hallway along which hung

many paintings and old photographs. She
stopped to examine a few and thought she
recognized Uncle Jim as a young man.
He was amongst a group of young people
who were having a picnic in the garden.
Everyone was laughing and she thought it
looked like a happy scene.

Further along the hallway, Charlotte
came to a strange-looking door which
creaked open after a couple of pushes.
Behind the door was a
winding staircase. It
looked so mysterious
that Charlotte
felt she must
climb the steps
and see what
was at the top.
The stairs wound
around and around
and Charlotte realized

that she must be inside the tower she had
seen on her arrival. At the top she came to
yet another door. She stood outside it for a
couple of moments and realized with some
surprise that she felt a little bit nervous.
The door was old and stiff. It hadn't been
opened for many years. Charlotte gave it a
couple of shoves and finally it opened and
she almost fell headlong into the room.

Charlotte stood there, feeling slightly
dizzy, her eyes adjusting to the darkness.
She went to the windows and drew back
a pair of curtains, which were thick with
dust. The room became slightly lighter
as the daylight filtered in. She looked
out of the window and tried to make out
the surrounding garden, but it seemed
shadowy and difficult to see. She turned
her attention back to the room. It had
clearly once belonged to a child. The
faded wallpaper had a nautical theme

and was patterned with sailing boats and anchors. Beside the window there was an old armchair. Charlotte curled up in it, suddenly feeling rather sleepy.

The next thing Charlotte knew, she was woken by what felt like a tap on her shoulder. She looked up from the chair, and had to squint because the room was bright now. Everything seemed newer and more colourful. The sailing boats on the wallpaper seemed so vibrant she could almost smell sea air. She looked out at the garden, wondering what time of day it was, and to her amazement saw that a thick blanket of snow had covered everything. And then from behind her she heard a boy laughing. Thinking her brothers had tracked her down she turned around, ready with a snappy comment. But instead she found herself looking at a boy of about her own age.

"I say," said the strange mystery boy in an old-fashioned accent. "You fell asleep in my favourite chair!"

"Oh…um…sorry," replied Charlotte, "I was just exploring. I didn't know this was anyone's room. Uncle Jim didn't tell me that any children lived here."

"Well I do and this is my room," answered the boy firmly, but in a friendly way that made Charlotte want to know all about him.

"Have you come to stay for Christmas?" asked the boy. "I do hope so. It would be wizard to have a fellow adventurer on board." Charlotte had never heard anyone talk like this before. What an unusual visit this was turning out to be!

Charlotte explained to the boy that she hadn't really wanted to spend Christmas here; it seemed as if there would be nothing to do stuck away in the middle of nowhere.

"Nothing to do!" exclaimed the boy. "Why, there's always plenty to do around here old girl." Charlotte wasn't sure that she liked being called an old girl, but she was very curious to know what it was that kept him so busy, and so she listened on attentively to what he had to say.

"Look," instructed the boy, pointing into a distant hedge, "there are robins nesting there. I like to leave food out

for them; the ground gets too frozen for
the little things to dig for worms in this
weather. You can help me make them
a new bird feeder if you like!" Charlotte
thought to herself that might be quite fun.

"Now look to the right of the hedge,"
continued the boy enthusiastically. "See
that clearing? That is the best place in
the garden to make a den!" Charlotte had
never actually made a den before but it did
sound like a laugh.

"You have to wrap up jolly warm," he
went on, "but then on Christmas Eve the
grown-ups can help to make a campfire
and we can toast marshmallows!"

"Marshmallows? Mmm, that sounds
alright,"nodded Charlotte.

"Why yes, what better way to look
out for old Santa Claus?" the boy replied
with a cheeky wink. "Of course we shan't
spot him, but it keeps the younger chaps

amused!" Charlotte thought how much her small brothers would enjoy that.

"First things first, though," said the boy suddenly. "We must build a snowman. It usually snows up here at Christmas, and when it does we always build a snowman and decorate him with holly and ivy from the front of the house." Charlotte and the boy agreed that first thing tomorrow, that's exactly what they would do.

Charlotte had no idea how long she had been up in the turret room, but she was beginning to feel hungry so she guessed it must have been some time.

"I really must go and find my family," said Charlotte as she walked across the room to the door. "Are you coming with me? I could eat a horse…" But when she turned back round to look for the boy there was no sign of him.

"Cheeky monkey!" she thought to

herself. "I expect I'll see him later."

Charlotte found her family just where she had left them, only now it was getting dark outside.

"Uncle Jim," asked Charlotte, "will you help us make a bonfire tomorrow, for Christmas Eve?"

"A bonfire?" he replied, puzzled.

"Yes, you know… to toast marshmallows and wait for Santa Claus," she went on.

"Well I never did!" said Uncle Jim, amazed. "Whoever told you about that? I haven't had a Christmas Eve bonfire since I was a young boy. It used to be a tradition in this house. We used to have such fun!" Then Charlotte told Uncle Jim all about the boy she had met in the tower and about the robins nesting and the best place in the garden to make a den.

"And of course," she added, "we

must make a snowman first and decorate him with holly and ivy."

"Oh yes! Can we make a snowman…if it snows of course," chipped in her brothers.

"What do you mean? Of course it has snowed," said Charlotte as she made her way towards the window. "I saw everything already covered in lovely white snow…Oh!"

Charlotte felt very confused. There was not a flake of snow anywhere, but hadn't she just seen it from upstairs?

"Hmm, the thing is there isn't a boy living in the

house, not any more," Uncle Jim explained thoughtfully.

"Perhaps you were tired after the trip, love. Maybe you fell asleep and dreamed all this," said her mum. Charlotte rushed back to the little turret room, this time with her brothers eagerly behind her, but there was nobody there. The walls looked faded again and when she called out, her voice just bounced off the walls back into the empty room.

The next day Charlotte woke up determined to find out whether she had been dreaming or not. She was sure she hadn't imagined everything. She wanted to go and see if there were any robins nesting in the hedge and she thought that perhaps her brothers might like to make a den. They could collect wood for a bonfire, too. When she looked out of her window she was thrilled to see that it really had snowed.

She rushed downstairs to see if anyone else was awake, and found everyone was up before her, eating breakfast.

"It's snowed! It's snowed!" sang her brothers as they jumped around the room with excitement.

"It usually snows up here at Christmas, and when it does we always used to build a snowman," said Uncle Jim.

"That's exactly what we'll do, and we'll decorate him with holly and ivy from the front of the house. Come on, everyone! There's loads to do!" added Charlotte.

Later that evening, as she sat wrapped up warm in front of a wonderful Christmas Eve bonfire with her family for company, Charlotte thought this was the best Christmas ever.

"Thank you for making the day such fun," smiled Uncle Jim. "I don't know how you did it, Charlotte, but it was just like old times when I was a child. It feels as if the old place has…well…come alive again! Its Christmas spirit has returned!"

"I think I may have met that Christmas spirit," smiled Charlotte to herself. Later she crept up into the turret and whispered "Thanks," into the empty room. She was sure she heard a faint whisper in return,

"Any time, old girl! Happy Christmas!"

An Unforgettable Performance

by Kath Jewitt

"Can I a bit of hush, please?" cried Mrs Dunwoody (or Dotty D, as the pupils of Mountbank School liked to call their eccentric teacher).

The noise levels in the school hall didn't change, but Mrs Dunwoody just carried on speaking. "Welcome, welcome, welcome!" she cried, clapping her hands. "Welcome to the auditions for the school Christmas play. It really is quite wonderful to see so many of you! This year I have great plans for our humble little performance. This year, it's going to be truly magnificent – a Christmas extravaganza, a visual feast! This year, it's going to be …."

"What IS it going to be?" a boy called Hamish burst out impatiently from the back of the hall.

Mrs Dunwoody smiled. "I'm glad you asked. This year, our school Christmas play is going to be unforgettable! It's going to be … Cinderella!"

There was lots of unimpressed muttering.

"What's so unforgettable about that?" whispered Bella, who was standing next to Hamish. "It's boring …"

"I know what you're thinking!" cried Mrs Dunwoody. "Cinderella isn't the most original story to chose. But this year I have a secret ingredient, something that will take our performance to new heights. Something that we've never tried before …"

At last, Mrs Dunwoody had her pupils' attention.

"What is it, Miss?" they chorused. "Tell

us, Miss!"

But Mrs Dunwoody would give nothing away.

"You'll just have to wait and see!" she smiled mysteriously. "Now, come along everybody. Let's get this audition started."

Early the next morning, Mrs Dunwoody pinned the results of the audition on the school notice board. Hamish and Bella were the first to see the list. They peered at it hopefully.

"Cinderella….Milly Baker, Prince Charming…Josh Jenkins, the Ugly Sisters …Sam Batty and Simon Wall," read Bella slowly. The list went on and on, but there was no sign of her name, or even Hamish's for that matter. Finally, at the very bottom, she found what she was looking for.

"Here we are," she sighed. "Props … Hamish Hunt and Bella Williams. Not again! We did that last year."

"Why do we always get the boring jobs?" complained Hamish. "You'd make a much better Cinderella than wimpy Milly Baker. She's even frightened of the school mice! It's not fair."

"Fairness has nothing to do with it," breezed Mrs Dunwoody, appearing from nowhere. "It's all about the right person for the right job. That's why I chose you."

"But we did props last year!" moaned Hamish.

"Exactly," said their teacher. "I need experienced people who won't be put off by a challenge."

"A pumpkin and a glass slipper ..." muttered Bella. "What's so challenging about that?"

"Ahh!" interrupted Mrs Dunwoody. "But what about the live animals?"

Hamish and Bella exchanged glances. "Live animals?" they repeated. "What live animals would those be?"

Mrs Dunwoody smiled triumphantly.
"It's my secret ingredient," she announced.
"With a little help from the special effects
team, the fairy godmother will turn a
pumpkin, and the school mice, into a
coach and horses right in front of the
audience."

"But we can't have horses on stage!"
cried Hamish, who was struggling to get his
head round the idea. "There's not enough

room up there!"

Mrs Dunwoody looked calmly at Hamish. "Of course not, Hamish. That would be silly. We're going to use goats."

"But goats look nothing like horses!" blurted out Bella.

Mrs Dunwoody would not be put off. "Have you never heard of artistic licence, Bella?" she asked. "The goats will look magnificent from where the audience is sitting!" And with that, she marched off down the corridor.

It wasn't long before Mrs Dunwoody's secret ingredient was the talk of the school.

"I knew she was dotty," sniggered Josh Jenkins. "But I think she's really lost it this time. Surely, she can't be serious!"

But Dotty D was serious, as the pupils soon discovered.

At the first rehearsal, Mrs Dunwoody announced that arrangements had been made to borrow six white goats from the local petting zoo.

"The animals will only make an appearance on the actual night," she explained. "In rehearsals, Bella and Hamish can stand in for them. We can use an empty cage for the mice until the performance."

Hamish and Bella were not impressed with being cast as goats, but there was no time to argue about it. There was far too much to do – like designing all the costumes. And that was just for starters. They had to get to grips with the special effects, paint all the background scenery, and build a giant papier mâché pumpkin-shaped coach.

The weeks running up to the big night just seemed to whizz by. Nobody had time to worry much about goats and mice until the final rehearsal. Then Mrs Dunwoody decided to talk everyone through the live animal scene one last time.

"Listen carefully, everyone," she shouted, clapping her hands. "This is what's going to happen. When the fairy godmother asks for mice, Cinderella will fetch the cage from the theatre wings."

"But Miss...I HATE mice!" piped up Milly Baker, who was playing Cinderella.

"Don't fuss, dear," frowned Mrs Dunwoody. "You won't have to touch them. They'll be in their cage. Now where was I? Ah, yes. Then comes the tinkling music from the orchestra. The fairy godmother waves her wand. Then Hamish will pour water into the tray of dry ice to make a smoke screen, while Bella removes the mouse cage. Then the coachmen will lead on the goats, pulling Cinderella's coach through the magical haze! Is everybody clear?"

"But how do we know the animals won't get stage fright?" asked Hamish, who still wasn't convinced.

Mrs D smiled. "The school mice are used to children and the goats see crowds of people everyday at the zoo. Everything will be just fine," she replied.

It all sounded so simple. Even the Head teacher, who had his doubts about the 'secret ingredient' was impressed. "It looks like we're all set for a wonderful performance tomorrow night," he congratulated Mrs Dunwoody. "You seem to have thought of everything."

But Mrs Dunwoody hadn't quite thought of everything. She hadn't, for example, thought about what would happen when six hungry goats had to wait in the school corridor with a giant papier mâché pumpkin coach. But she soon found out when they arrived. The greedy creatures took one look at the giant vegetable and made a bee-line for it. And there was nothing that Bella or Hamish could do to hold them back!

"Whoa!" cried Bella, as three determined goats dragged her up the corridor.

"Someone rescue the coach!" yelled

Hamish, as the biggest goat began to munch on the pumpkin.

And it got worse. Much worse. After taking a bite out of Cinderella's coach, the crazy goats moved on to her broom. Then they attacked the lacy skirt of her ballgown, which was hanging up in the theatre wings. By the time Bella, Hamish and Mrs Dunwoody had managed to catch them again, the goats had left a trail of half-nibbled props. And the play was just about to start.

"How are we going to keep them under control on the stage?" panted Bella, trying to stop one goat from snaffling a bag of blueberry muffins that Mrs Dunwoody had bought.

Hamish grinned. "I think I've got the answer," he said, holding out a yummy muffin. At once, the greedy creature snatched the cake from his hand and began to munch with a blissful expression on its face.

"Well done!" cried Mrs Dunwoody. "Our little problem is solved! I'm sure everything will be fine now."

But everything was far from fine. Suddenly, without warning, Bella gave a shriek and dived on the floor.

"Get up, Bella!" demanded Mrs Dunwoody crossly. "This is no time for messing about. The curtain goes up in five minutes."

"I'm not messing about!" replied Bella, holding up a small white ball of fur. "I'm catching the school mice! The goats must have kicked open their cage." And she pointed to the empty cage on the floor.

"Oh no!" groaned Hamish. "We've got to catch them before Milly finds out! She's terrified of mice!"

Even Mrs Dunwoody could see that this was a serious problem.

"Catch them quickly. Don't tell anyone

what you are doing!" she urged. "If Milly finds out, we'll NEVER get her on stage."

And so, as the curtain went up and the play began, so did the hunt for the school mice. It wasn't easy secretly finding five small rodents in a hall full of people, but it is amazing what you can do when you have to. And it wasn't long before Bella spotted one, scurrying along the bottom edge of the stage. Quick as a flash, she got

down on all fours and crawled after it, whispering apologies to the people in the front row seats. Just as Bella cornered her prey, there was a loud crash from the orchestra pit, and a muffled cry of triumph. Hamish had found two more!

It was Mrs Dunwoody who found the fourth mouse, curled up fast asleep in an ugly sister's wig, while the fifth mouse finally turned up in Cinderella's glass slipper. But the sixth and final mouse was nowhere to be found. "You two had better go and get everything ready in the wings," said a flustered Mrs Dunwoody to Bella and Hamish. "The live animal scene is next. I'm sure the last mouse will turn up safely sooner or later."

In fact, it turned up sooner – just as the big scene was beginning! Bella and Hamish watched helplessly from the wings, as the cheeky little creature walked calmly across the front of the stage, scaled Cinderella's broom and jumped into her apron pocket, without her even noticing.

"We've got to get that apron before Milly puts her hands in the pocket," breathed Hamish, "or we're going to be in BIG trouble!"

Then he had a brainwave. He grabbed the fairy godmother, who was just about to step on stage.

"Get Milly to give you her apron, then pass it to me!" he whispered.

The fairy godmother looked confused. "But how?" she asked. "It's not in the script!"

"I don't know!" hissed Bella, almost pushing the confused fairy onto the stage. "Tell her to hang it up or something. JUST DO IT!"

Less than a minute later the apron was safely delivered into Hamish's hands. Bella peered anxiously in the pocket, and breathed a sigh of relief. The mouse was still there!

"Just in time," grinned Hamish, popping the mouse back in the cage.

"Listen!"

Tinkling music drifted up from the orchestra pit, as the fairy godmother prepared to do her magic. It was time for Mrs Dunwoody's big moment!

And what a moment it was. Everything went perfectly to plan. Hamish's smoke screen worked brilliantly, and the goats (who were stuffed with blueberry muffins and props by now) behaved themselves with impressive good manners. Even Milly managed not to scream when she held the cage of mice.

"Thank goodness she never found out what happened," sniggered Hamish, listening to the wild applause. "The whole thing would have been a disaster."

"Don't exaggerate, Hamish," scolded Mrs Dunwoody, who seemed to have recovered her usual enthusiasm. "I would say our performance is going to be a runaway success. I don't know what all the fuss was about!"

Bella and Hamish laughed. "Well, we can all agree about one thing," said Bella. "It's certainly been an unforgettable Christmas performance!"

Friends for Christmas

by Hettie Bingham

Tess and Harry were too busy arguing to eat their tea, and their mum was sighing with exasperation.

"I just don't know why you two are always arguing with each other," she said. "It's not as if you don't have anything in common. You are twins after all!" But she knew her words would do no good. Tess and Harry were always at loggerheads, and in the short time they had been at the table they had argued about what TV programmes they liked, who was best at catching a ball and who had the most food on their plate.

When the doorbell went Mum was

quite relieved, especially when she opened the door to Emma.

"Hi, Emma! Who are you calling for today?" she asked the visitor. "Tess and Harry are both in."

Emma was friends with Harry and Tess, great friends with both of them… just not both at the same time. How could she be when the twins were always arguing about something or other?

"Er, hello, Mrs Davies," replied Emma a little nervously. "I've come to get Harry this time. It's Thursday, so it's our basketball club."

Every Thursday evening, Emma and Harry played basketball together for the local under 11s team. Tess didn't want to join in. She preferred trampolining, which she did with Emma every Monday evening.

"Bye Tess," called out Emma, as she and Harry left. "See you later."

Emma loved spending time with her two friends, but she really wished they could all spend time together. It would soon be Christmas and there were so many exciting treats in store. Why couldn't they all share them together? But Emma knew it was no use. Her friends argued so much it was no fun at all being with them both at the same time.

Christmas Day was drawing closer and the holidays had already begun. There was plenty to keep Emma and her friends busy. On Saturday she was going to see a Christmas pantomime with Harry. The following Monday she was going round to make gingerbread tree decorations with Tess. It would all be so much fun, Emma could hardly wait.

But then disaster struck. On the Saturday of the Christmas pantomime, Emma awoke with a tickly feeling in her throat. She hoped it would get better during the morning, but before long her head began to pound and she developed a high temperature.

"Sorry love," said Emma's mum, "you'll have to go back to bed. No pantomime for you today." Emma felt wretched: the last thing she wanted was to be ill over Christmas. She phoned Harry to break the news.

"Sorry Harry, you'll have to find someone else to take to the panto, I'm just not feeling well enough," she croaked down the phone.

"But Emma, you can't be ill over Christmas… it's just not fair," said Harry, his voice trailing away with disappointment.

Harry felt very fed up. He had been looking forward to his outing and now who would go with him? But most of all he felt sorry for Emma; of all the times to be ill she couldn't have picked a worse one.

"What's up with you, slug face?" taunted Tess when she noticed Harry still sitting miserably by the phone. Now, usually Harry would have had a snappy reply up his sleeve and it would be the start of yet another argument, but not today.

"It's poor Emma," he replied glumly. "She's in bed with the flu and she can't come to the pantomime. I shouldn't think you'll be making gingerbread with her on Monday either. She didn't sound very well at all."

The twins felt very gloomy, so much so that they forgot to bicker. They were both fed up that their treats were spoiled, but they were more sorry for Emma, whose Christmas might be ruined.

"I wish I could think of a way to make Emma feel better," sighed Tess.

"Me too," replied Harry. For once the twins actually agreed on something...and it didn't feel too bad either!

"It can't be helped," said Tess and Harry's mum, popping her head around the door. "You can tell Emma all about the pantomime Harry, and Tess, I'll help you make gingerbread tomorrow and you can

take some round to Emma on Monday. That'll cheer her up!" But Tess and Harry weren't convinced. Christmas was so special, surely it would take more than that to make Emma feel happier.

The twins ate their lunch in silence, not because they'd argued but because they were both thinking hard about ways to cheer up their friend.

"Are you ready for the pantomime, Harry?" asked Mum when the twins had finished eating. "Who have you decided to take with you?" Harry hadn't even begun to think about that. He had more important things on his mind.

"Tess…" asked Harry slowly, "I don't suppose you'd like to come to the panto with me?"

"Me? But last week you said you'd rather eat worms than sit through a panto with me!" replied Tess, astonished.

"Well, things are different now, and anyway it'll be more fun for Emma if we can both tell her about it. We can act out the funniest bits for her," explained Harry.

"OK," agreed Tess.

The pantomime was great fun, and when Tess and Harry's mum arrived to take them home she was pleased to see the children laughing together as they left the theatre. It was only when the two were sound asleep that night that she realized her terrible twins hadn't argued all day.

The next day was Sunday and, as promised, Mum was helping Tess to make gingerbread tree decorations. She poured the sticky dough out onto the floury surface and Tess began to roll it flat. She made star shapes and Christmas tree shapes and squares that she would decorate to look like presents. After a little while Harry came into the kitchen.

"Can I cut out some shapes, too?" he asked. Tess was about to complain that this was her dough, and it was her own surprise for Emma. But then she thought that perhaps Emma would be pleased if Harry made some, too.

"All right," answered Tess, still a little grudgingly, "you can make a few."

"Great! Thanks, sis!" said Harry as he eagerly began to cut out circle shapes in the gingerbread. "I'm making gingerbread basketballs. Emma will love them!"

Mum carefully slid the baking tray into the oven. A short while later the gingerbread was perfectly cooked to a lovely golden brown, and a sweet, spicy smell filled the kitchen. Harry and Tess decorated the gingerbread shapes with icing sugar and wrapped them up carefully before bedtime, ready to take to Emma the next day.

"Well I never…" thought Harry and Tess's surprised parents that night, "…another peaceful day!"

The next morning Harry and Tess could hardly wait to see their poorly friend.

"I hope Emma's feeling better today," sighed Tess.

"Yes, it's Christmas Eve tomorrow. She's got to get well in time to enjoy that," added Harry.

At Emma's house, the twins raced upstairs to her bedroom where they found their friend propped up in bed reading a book.

"Hello," she croaked, mustering up

the biggest smile she could under the circumstances. She felt a little nervous to see the twins together. A row was the last thing she needed right now!

But Emma needn't have worried because Harry and Tess were so pleased to see their friend that an argument was the last thing on their minds. They immediately started to describe the panto they had seen together and she listened attentively as they told her all about it. They even acted out a scene with the custard pie, using one of Emma's cushions! When they had finished, the twins collapsed in fits of giggles on Emma's bed and the three of them laughed so much that Emma's dad came in to see what was going on.

"I thought you were supposed to be ill," teased Emma's dad.

"Actually, I think I'm beginning to feel a bit better," answered Emma, "perhaps I'll be well in time for Christmas after all!"

"Well enough for some gingerbread?" enquired Tess as she presented the box that she and Harry had carefully packed the night before.

"We made it together," said Harry.

"Well, I did most of the work…" Tess began to argue, but then the twins looked at each other and smiled, "but Harry helped a lot and it was great fun," she added.

Emma couldn't believe her eyes! This was the best tonic and the best Christmas present she could have hoped for: her two best friends getting on together at last.

"We made lots of different shapes," Tess told Emma. "If you're feeling better tomorrow you can hang them on your tree!"

"But I think we should taste one or two now, just to make sure they're alright!" added Harry, cheekily.

The next day, Emma did feel a lot better, and she decorated her Christmas tree with the gingerbread decorations. By Christmas Day she was completely well again and had a lovely time, opening her presents and feeling very jolly.

On Boxing Day Emma had arranged to go to Harry and Tess's house. What if the twins had gone back to their old ways and were arguing again? She rang the doorbell and waited anxiously for it to be answered. Then she heard footsteps, two sets of them, charging towards her. The door swung open to reveal two smiling faces.

"Emma!" the twins cried out together. "Come on in and see the fabulous presents we got!"

Emma liked Harry's new computer game. Tess's art set was amazing, too.

"I can't show you my best Christmas

present," smiled Emma, "or, come to think
of it, maybe I can. Follow me!" She led
the twins into the hall and pointed at the
mirror that was hanging there.

"Look in the mirror!" she giggled.

Tess and Harry were puzzled for a

moment, but then they did as she said and looked in the mirror … at their own two smiling faces, side by side!

One Spooky Christmas

by Gaby Goldsack

Christmas was coming and Grantley Manor had opened after redevelopment to turn it into a smart hotel. It was swarming with jolly guests who had come to celebrate the festive season. The dining room was decked out in a dazzling display of tinsel and holly. An enormous bauble-covered Christmas tree towered over the guests as they were welcomed at Reception. The kitchen shelves groaned under the weight of Christmas goodies, and everywhere you went in the hotel people were laughing and smiling, and shouting "Merry Christmas!". It seemed that just about everyone was full of the festive spirit. Everyone that is, except for Harold…

Harold was sulking in a dark, dusty and rather smelly forgotten corner of the attic at the top of the old house. Every now and then he would rattle his chains and wail as loudly as he could. For, you see, Harold was no ordinary person. He was a ghost, and not a very happy ghost at that. He had lived at Grantley Manor long before it was a hotel, and he didn't like all the new visitors.

"Cheer up, Harold," sang Skeleton, Harold's ghostly best friend. "It might never happen!"

"But it already has," wailed Harold. "I'm dead in case you haven't noticed, and my old home has been turned into a horrible hotel."

"Well, at least Christmas is just around the corner," croaked Tut, the Egyptian mummy ghost. "Everyone loves

Christmas. It's full of laughter and joy, and goodwill to all men."

"Ha," snorted Harold. "Goodwill to all MEN perhaps, but us spooks aren't going to have much of a Christmas now this place has been invaded by snotty, feeble-minded guests. I can't even wail and rattle my chains in public without some idiot screaming the place down. Some Christmas I'm going to have!"

"Oh, it's not so bad…" began Skeleton. But before he could continue, his voice was drowned out by a blast of jingly music wafting through the floorboards from below. The hotel guests were playing Christmas carols at full volume.

Soon the other spooks of Grantley Manor floated into the attic to sit miserably beside Harold.

"This place is ruined," sighed Sir Hauntalot, the ghostly knight. "It just hasn't been the same since Mr and Mrs Jones replaced all the lovely old rotting shutters with frilly curtains and turned it into a beastly place for humans to stay."

"Too true," agreed Harold. "I just don't feel comfortable with all those horrid guests poking around the place. I don't know what it is about humans but they give me the creeps. I barely leave the attic nowadays for fear of running into one of them."

"Yes," added Skeleton, shuddering so hard at the thought of humans that his bones rattled and his skull spun round and round in circles. "They seem to be constantly taking showers and changing their clothes. Yuck! It's just not decent."

The unhappy ghouls started to wail and groan above the noise of the carols. It just didn't seem fair that their home had been invaded and they were forced to hide in the gloomy attic. They were still wailing and grinding their teeth five minutes later when the Headless Lady floated in through the wall, holding her head under her arm.

"What's all this?" laughed the Headless Lady, who always managed to have a smile on her face despite having her head inconveniently chopped off many years ago. "Are you having a ghostly singalong?"

"Of course not," sniffed Harold. "We're just feeling down in the dumps because the place is swarming with silly guests and our Christmas has been ruined. That's all."

"Oh, come on. Pull yourself together! Look, I can do it!" giggled the Headless Lady, balancing her head on her neck. "Spirited spooks like us can't let a bunch of namby-pamby humans get the better of us. After all, it's our Christmas, too. I know! Why don't we have a Christmas party of our own?"

The spooks stopped their weeping and wailing and looked at the Headless Lady with respect.

"What a brilliant idea," said Harold

with the hint of a ghostly smile.

"We could have beastly brew and creepy crisps," cried Tut. "And fried bats wings and eerie eyeballs," added Skeleton, shaking with excitement.

"We can have old-time dancing," roared Sir Hauntalot. "Hundreds of years old, in fact!" He leapt to his feet and his armour clanged and creaked as he gave his friends a noisy demonstration of his favourite dance from centuries ago.

And so the ghosts of Grantley Manor began to organize an unearthly Christmas Eve party. They were so busy planning what to do and what to eat, that the hotel guests hardly bothered them at all and before they knew it Christmas Eve had arrived. As midnight approached, each of them stood in the attic dressed in their finest rags. Then on the stroke of midnight, Harold banged a rusty old gong and cried, "LET THE PARTY BEGIN!"

As soon as the words had left his pale blue lips, the spooks began to drift out of the attic towards the Grand Hall. Luckily all the guests were tucked up safely in bed, so the spooky spirits didn't get any nasty human surprises along the way. Once in the Hall, Tut chanted an ancient mummy's spell and a table full of spooky snacks and devilish drinks appeared before them. The hotel's glittering Christmas decorations disappeared, to be replaced with dusty cobwebs and hideous pumpkin lanterns. The colourful baubles on the giant Christmas tree were replaced with grinning skulls and enormous eyeballs. Then the Headless Lady sat down at the piano and began to play a creepy Christmas carol. Soon everyone was joining in and the hotel shook to the beat of wretched wails and beastly bangs.

The ghosts were having a wonderfully gruesome time and they were enjoying themselves so much, that nobody heard the first scream as one of the hotel guests realized that something scary was afoot. Soon, all the guests were running out of their rooms, panicking and shouting about the spine-chilling sounds they could hear. It was a complete mystery to them because, although they could hear the ghosties and ghoulies, they couldn't actually see them. Mr and Mrs Jones, the hotel owners, were doing their best to calm the terrified crowd.

"What was that rattling?" quacked Mr Brown from Room 6.

"Er…that will be the plumbing," said Mr Jones.

"What's that wailing?" cried Mrs Webb from Room 8.

"Um…the cat," said Mrs Jones, looking nervously around.

"And what about that ghostly song?" demanded Major Curnow from Room 4.

Mr and Mrs Jones looked at each

other in panic and both spoke at once.

"That's my mother," said Mr Jones.

"That's the wind," said Mrs Jones.

"Well I don't believe you," roared Major Curnow. "I think this place is

haunted, and I can't be doing with ghosts. I'm leaving this very minute." And, without waiting another second, he marched out of the front door.

Meanwhile, the spooks began to dance a ghostly conga, and began stamping their way around the hotel. As they wound up the stairs towards Mr and Mrs Jones and the guests, the banging and crashing got louder and louder. And so did the wails, groans and rattling of bones.

"W…w…what's that?" stuttered Mrs Jones, looking very frightened indeed.

"I've no idea," quivered Mr Jones, trying to hide behind his wife. "I just wish we could see what was making all the racket. I'm sure there's a perfectly good explanation."

As luck would have it, at that very moment, the magical light of a Christmas full moon shone through the hotel windows and Mr Jones's wish was granted. Suddenly, Mr and Mrs Jones and their quivering guests could see Harold and his pals in all their ghoulish glory.

"Ahhhhhhhh!" screamed Mrs Jones.

"Ahhhhhhhhhhh!" screamed Mr Jones.

"Ahhhhhhhhhhhhhh!" screamed all
the guests.

The spooks stood still and stared back
in horror.

"Ahhhhhhhhhhhh! Horrible humans!"
screamed Harold when he saw that Mrs
Jones was wearing a hideous hairnet
and a face-full of slippery cream. Then
all hell broke loose, as ghosties, ghoulies
and ghastly guesties began running in all
directions. Mr Jones ran through Harold.
Mrs Webb ran through the Headless Lady.
The spooks were scattered left, right and
centre as the humans stampeded out of the
front door.

"I'm never going to step foot in this
ghost-ridden hotel ever again," Mrs Jones
wailed.

"You ghastly ghosts can have it as far as I'm concerned. Good riddance to the lot of you!" Mr Jones shouted. And with that, he slammed the door and the spooks were left alone.

The Headless Lady was as white as a sheet and shivering. She couldn't believe that a horrible human had actually walked through her. Skeleton was so shaken up that his knee bones kept knocking together. Poor Tut, the mummy, had to rewind some of his bandages because he had begun to unwrap in all the chaos. No one said anything for a while, and then Harold began to do something very spooky indeed – he began to let out a low, long ghostly laugh.

"Whooooo-hoooooooo-hooooooooo!"

His chin wobbled and his blue lips trembled. He laughed so much that he fell to his wobbly knobbly knees in front of the enormous Christmas tree.

"That was brilliant!" he spluttered. "Did you see how scared the humans were?"

Soon all the ghostly friends were

laughing. Then Harold looked at the beautifully wrapped presents lying beneath the Christmas tree, and his eyes began to sparkle with excitement. He hadn't felt this good for centuries. He picked up a neatly wrapped parcel and passed it to Skeleton.

"Merry Christmas," he chuckled. "I think all these presents are ours now. In fact, this house and everything in it are ours once more. Something tells me that this is going to be the best Christmas ever!"

"Hurrah for us!" cried Sir Hauntalot, leaping up to lead his friends in another crazy ghost dance. "Shake those bones! Rattle those chains! Here comes Christmas, and it's going to be the creepiest one ever!'

The Christmas Wish

by Hettie Bingham

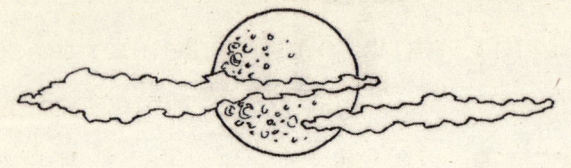

Tom watched sadly as the removal van pulled away and turned off round the corner, back to his old town and his old friends. He sat on the garden wall of his new house and looked at his toes, staring hard at them so that he didn't cry.

"Come on Tom, grab a box!" called his mum, who was busy carrying in the last few boxes, in the hope that she would find the one with the kettle in it.

Tom had not wanted to move house, especially not just before Christmas. All his old friends would be having lots of fun right now, going to parties and swapping cards in the school post box. Tom wondered if he'd get any cards at all this year.

"Don't worry Tom," his mum had said. "You'll make loads of new friends when you start school." But it wasn't that easy. Tom was rather shy and he didn't look forward to being the new boy one bit.

"Found it!" called Tom's mum, holding the kettle high in the air like a trophy, "Who wants a hot drink?" Tom walked slowly into his new house thinking it would take more than a hot drink to solve his problems.

The next day Tom was up bright and early to start school. He really hoped he would make some friends, even though there were only two days left before the holidays. When he found his new classroom, the teacher introduced him to everyone and, although the other children were very friendly, they were all too excited about Christmas to take the time to make proper friends with him. Tom ate his lunch alone that day, and the next day too. When school was finished he walked home slowly while the other children chattered excitedly around him.

That night, Tom stared out of his window. It was a clear, starry night and the winter moon was a beautiful pale yellow.

"Hello Moon," whispered Tom. "You're the same moon I've always looked at, aren't you. It's only me that's in a different place." Tom felt a little bit silly talking to the moon, but it did make him feel less lonely, so he carried on. "I wish I could find a new friend for Christmas," he sighed. "Can you help me find one, Moon?"

The next morning was the first day of the school holiday. Tom's dad had already left for his new job, the reason Tom had to move house in the first place. Tom's mum was busy painting the kitchen, holding a

paint brush in one hand and a piece of
toast in the other.

"Grab yourself some breakfast, love,"
she told Tom between mouthfuls, "and
then go and play. I've got lots to do today."

"Play?" replied Tom. "Who with? I
don't have any friends around here. There's
nothing to do. I'm bored."

"You'll find something to do, I'm sure,"
said his mum. "Go and explore outside!"
Tom couldn't think of a better idea, so after
eating a bowl of cereal he went out to look
around his new street.

Tom's new house was in a cul-de-sac,
which meant that it was nice and quiet.
No cars could pass through and only the
people who lived there would drive in and
out. The road itself was shaped a little bit
like a question mark, and inside the curved
part of it was a circle of grass which Tom
sat down on to see if anything interesting

would happen. He watched as the
postman delivered the mail. Then he saw
a lady arrive home with some shopping,
but nothing very interesting seemed to
be happening. He didn't spot any other
children.

Tom decided to stroll around the circle and back to see if he could spot any other signs of life. Just as he was walking past a house with a tall hedge, a cat popped out from beneath the gate and rubbed up against his legs.

"Hello puss!" said Tom affectionately, as the cat meowed and nuzzled her head against his hand. "You're a lovely cat aren't you? You'll be my friend even if nobody else will." As Tom continued to stroke the cat, he heard a strange sound coming from behind the hedge. It was a sort of squeaking noise and then a humming sound, a little bit like a robot.

"Hey puss, is that where you live? Do you know if there are any robots around here?" Tom asked the cat. The cat just meowed and looked up at him. Tom listened again. The strange noises had stopped, but now he thought he heard something else, a little giggle. He wanted to call out and see if someone was there, but he was too shy. He went home wondering what the noises could have been.

Tom ate lunch with his mum in a kitchen that was now half yellow and half pink. Mum told him that by the end of the day the pink would be completely gone and they would be basking in 'Sunshine Yellow' by supper time. Tom realized this meant that his mum would be busy for the rest of the day, so when he went out again he took a few things to keep himself busy. He packed binoculars (very handy for exploring new territory) and a note pad and pen, just in case he needed to write down anything important. He also took a torch for any dark corners he might encounter and a carton of juice and some chocolate biscuits. Now he was all set to explore properly.

First of all he sat on the circle of
grass and looked through his binoculars.
He started by pointing them at the top
of the road and then slowly swept them
down, across all of the houses, until he
saw the house with the high hedge where
he had seen the cat and heard the strange
robot sounds. He spent a few minutes
just looking and waiting for something to
happen, but nothing did. He walked slowly
and carefully towards the hedge so that he
could listen up close. There was a sudden
whirring sound and the cat shot out of the
hedge past his feet.

"Here kitty, kitty," whispered Tom,
trying to coax the cat back towards him.
The cat gave a little meow and then
strolled over to where he was sitting so that
Tom could stroke his head.

"Nice kitty. I wish you could talk, then
you could tell me all about the robot," said

Tom softly. It was then that he heard a giggling noise again. Tom really wished he was brave enough to go through the garden gate and get a good look behind the hedge, but he really was too shy. Then he had a clever idea. He rummaged through his bag and found the note pad and pencil he had packed earlier. He scribbled a note and tucked it into the cat's collar. The note read: *Hello, is there a robot there? I'd like to meet you. From Tom.*

Tom persuaded the cat to go back through the hedge, and he waited to see what would happen. After a while the cat came back out through the hedge. At first glance Tom thought it was his own note still tucked in the collar, but when he took a closer look he was thrilled to find it was a new note which read: *Come in and see!*

How mysterious! Tom was nervous, but he felt so curious that he managed to

find the confidence to walk through the
garden gate.

"Hello," he called out nervously. All
of a sudden a girl's head popped up from
behind a large evergreen shrub.

"Hello!" replied the girl cheerfully. "My
name's Kirsty."

"My name's
Tom and I've
just moved here,"
said Tom. "I don't
suppose you've
noticed any
robots," he added.

"Robots?"
asked the girl,
giggling.

"Yes, I'm sure I
heard some strange
noises coming from behind your hedge.
They sounded just like the kind of noises

that robots make."

Suddenly the noises started up again and Tom watched as Kirsty came gliding out from behind the bush in a fantastic-looking wheelchair! Suddenly everything made sense to Tom.

"I suppose my chair is a bit like a robot in a way," explained Kirsty. "It is electric, it does have wheels and it's certainly very helpful!"

Kirsty and Tom were soon chatting away like old friends. Tom explained that he had been feeling very lonely in his new house and that he hadn't had the chance to make friends at school yet. It turned out that Kirsty went to the same school as Tom and she promised to introduce him to everyone as soon as school started again. Meanwhile the two new friends tucked into Tom's supply of chocolate biscuits.

"It's great you've moved here," said

Kirsty happily. "There are no other children our age on this street and it can sometimes get a little bit lonely in the holidays."

"But not anymore," chipped in Tom.

"Promise you won't laugh if I tell you something?" said Kirsty, blushing slightly.

"All right," replied Tom. "What?"

"The other night I was looking out of

my window at the most beautiful winter moon and, well, it's a bit soppy really, but I made a wish."

"Oh, er, that does sound a bit soppy actually," said Tom, blushing a little bit himself. "What did you wish for?"

"A new friend in my street!" said Kirsty happily. "My Christmas wish came true."

"That's funny," replied Tom, "so did mine!"

The Battle of the Bulbs

by Gaby Goldsack

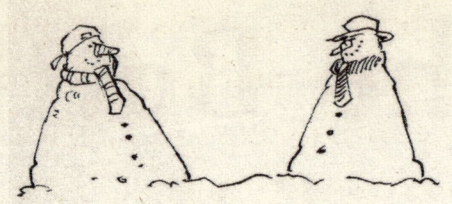

One snowy afternoon, just before Christmas, Jim Jones and Dom Webb were making snowmen in Dom's back garden.

"I've finished," cried Jim, as he plonked his dad's old gardening hat on his snowman's head.

"Yeah, well, mine's much bigger than yours," boasted Dom.

"So?" said Jim, punching Dom playfully in the arm.

"So, mine's the best, of course," laughed Dom.

Jim shrugged his shoulders and grinned. He knew his snowman was better but he saw no point in arguing. He and

Dom might be best mates but that didn't
stop them from being just the teeniest
bit competitive about…well, just about
everything. You see, Jim and Dom had lived
next door to each other forever and were
almost exactly the same age. Well, Dom
was one day older than Jim to be exact,
a fact that Dom never let Jim forget.

Jim was deciding whether or not
to pelt his friend with snowballs, when
there was a shout from his dad. He'd just
returned from shopping and was hauling a
huge box out of the boot of his car.

"Come and help me with this lot," he
called to Jim.

Jim and Dom rushed over to see what
he'd bought.

"Do you need a hand, Mr Jones?"
asked Dom.

"Er, no," replied Jim's dad, looking
a little shifty and awkward. "I think it's

probably best if you run along home now. Jim and I've got work to do."

Dom looked decidedly put out but did as he was told.

"What was that all about?" asked Jim, once his friend had disappeared inside his own house. "Is that box top secret or something?"

"You could say that," replied Mr Jones with a grin. "I've bought some new Christmas lights and I don't want Dom running off to tell his dad about them. You know how competitive Mr Webb is."

Jim nodded his head knowingly. Dom's dad was even more competitive than Dom. If Jim's dad got a new lawnmower Mr Webb would shoot out and buy a bigger and better one.

Jim and his dad spent the rest of the afternoon hanging a long string of icicle lights all around their front porch. Jim couldn't wait until darkness fell so that they could switch them on. And, being mid-winter, they didn't have long to wait. At dusk, Jim, his young sister Katy and their mum gathered outside the porch, while Mr Jones stood beside the switch.

"Ta-da," cried Mr Jones, as the lights went on.

"Ooooh," cried Katy.

"Ahhh," gasped Mum.

"Brilliant," laughed Jim. "They're the best yet."

They were all standing around admiring the way the lights shimmered, rippled and flashed on and off, when there was a bright flash of light from next door.

"What was that?" cried Mr Jones.

"It came from the Webb's house," cried Jim. The Jones family rushed over to see what was going on, and they were in for a bit of a shock. Dom and his dad had also

had a very busy afternoon hanging lights of
their own, lights that were not only much
bigger and brighter than Jim's and his
dad's, but also much more colourful. They

covered the whole front of their house.

"I don't believe it," gasped Jim.

"Flash bunch," cried Dad. "Come on,
everyone. Let's go inside."

Jim and his dad marched into their

house, feeling thoroughly outshone. But Mrs Jones and Katy stayed outside to admire the lights.

The following day, Jim and his dad rushed to the big DIY store in town and bought a trolley load of colourful Christmas lights in all shapes and sizes. Then they hurried home and set to work straight away. Jim had drawn a plan the night before, so they knew exactly what needed to be done. While they strung lights all over the fence in front of the house, Mum and Katy supplied them with a steady stream of tea and hot chocolate to keep them warm. Then, when darkness fell once more, the Jones family gathered round for the grand switching on.

"One, two, three, GO!" shouted Jim. Mr Jones flicked the switch and the lights flashed on to reveal the outline of an enormous snowman, complete with a flashing nose and twinkling eyes, sitting among a shower of sparkling snowflakes.

"Wow," cried Katy, clapping.

"Well done," said Mrs Jones.

"Not bad, not bad at all if I do say so myself," smiled Mr Jones, clapping Jim across his shoulder. Next door the sitting room curtains twitched.

"Look," whispered Jim, nudging his dad in the ribs. "We're being watched. Shall we pretend we haven't seen them?"

"No way," grinned Mr Jones. "Smile and wave, smile and wave. They must be gutted now we've got the best lights in the street."

"Yes," laughed Jim. "Their display does look kind of pathetic in comparison." As Jim and his dad made a huge performance of waving to Dom and his dad, Katy and Mum crept inside.

"Why are they so competitive?" Katy

asked Mum.

"I've no idea," sighed Mum, shaking her head sadly.

That night, Jim went to bed with a big smile on his face. As much as he liked Dom, he liked it even more when he beat him at something. The Webbs would have to do something really spectacular to make their lights even better than the Jones's. However, when Jim looked out of his bedroom window the following morning, he didn't feel quite so sure of himself. Dom and his dad must have got up really early and were now busy draping their whole house in thousands and thousands of lights.

"Dad," cried Jim, almost falling down the stairs in his rush to get down.

"I know, son," called his dad. "Grab your coat. We're going shopping."

"What for?" asked Mum, appearing in

the kitchen still half asleep.

"LIGHTS, of course," cried Dad and, without any further explanation, he and Jim were gone.

Jim and his dad returned a few hours later with a car full of lights. They'd driven around town buying up as many as they could.

"There won't be any lights left for Dom and his dad to buy," laughed Jim, as they hung bulbs here and draped bulbs there. "Our house is going to have the best Christmas lights in town."

But that evening, at lighting-up time, Jim wasn't so certain. Their lights might look great, but Dom and his dad had managed to create a dazzling display. They had eight reindeer pulling Santa's sleigh across the front of the house. There were huge twinkling stars on the sides of the house and strings of flashing lights around every door and window.

"Why didn't we think of that?"
muttered Jim.

"Aha, but they didn't think of creating

a picture in their trees, did they? And that
Christmas train on our roof and Santa
climbing down our chimney look really...
Oh what's the word I'm thinking of?"

muttered Mr Jones.

"Vulgar?" suggested Mrs Jones.

"Gross?" suggested Katy.

"NO," gasped Dad, looking rather surprised. "I was about to say classy."

"Yes, they do look classy," agreed Jim. "And they look miles better than the Webbs'." But really and truly, deep down, he wasn't so sure and neither was his dad. So that night, when everyone in the street was tucked up safely in bed, they crept out of bed and did something a little bit naughty. They removed just one tiny little bulb from the Webbs' marvellous display and replaced it with a broken one.

The next evening, when Mr Webb went to turn on the lights his house remained in darkness. As Jim and his dad stood back to admire their sparkling display, Dom and his dad set about finding out what could be wrong. They checked the fuses, which were okay. They checked the connections. They were okay, too. Then began the painfully slow job of checking each and every bulb, because Mr Webb said that just one bad bulb could stop the whole lot working. After what seemed like hours, Mr Webb found the culprit, a tiny little bulb high up on top of the chimney.

"I suspect sabotage," Mr Webb told Dom sternly.

"What shall we do about it?" asked Dom.

"Don't worry," replied Mr Webb, eyeing up the Jones's Christmas display. "I've just had a wonderful idea."

Meanwhile, inside Jim's house the mums were having a cup of cocoa.

"I don't know who is worse, the boys or their fathers," sighed Mrs Jones.

"It's hard to imagine that they're all the best of friends really," said Mrs Webb.

"Let's hope it's all over by Christmas Day. Otherwise I can't imagine how we're going to be able to share our usual Christmas dinner."

"Ah, these things have a way or sorting themselves out," said Mrs Jones. "The

Christmas spirit normally wins in the end."

"I hope so," said Katy. "I've never seen

them all being so competitive. It just can't
get any worse than this." But she couldn't
have been more wrong, for the following
night things got much worse. When the
two houses lit up, both families gasped.
Somebody had tinkered with the Jones's
tree lights so that they now read 'Messy
Christmas' rather than 'Merry Christmas'.

"Now that's really dirty," yelled Mr
Jones, fuming so much that you could
almost see smoke pouring out of his ears.
"This means war." And so the Battle of the
Bulbs began.

Each night after that, as darkness fell
and the Christmas lights were switched
on, all the neighbours would gather round
to find out what would happen next.
Bulbs would go missing. Lights would
mysteriously flick on and off when they
shouldn't. Reindeer would lose their
antlers. And one night, Jim and his dad's

chimney-climbing Santa was transformed into a masked crook.

By Christmas Eve, news of the Battle of the Bulbs had spread and people from up and down the street had come to watch. They stood around and marvelled as lights flicked on, flashed off, dazzled and dimmed. Then, when everyone was least expecting it, there was a puff of blue smoke, followed by an enormous BANG, and all the lights went out.

"Hey, what's happening now?" cried Mrs Webb, dashing out of the house that had been plunged into darkness.

"Yes, what have you done?" wailed Mrs Jones from her pitch-black kitchen. "Now we've got no power at all."

"It's all his fault," yelled Mr Jones, pointing at Mr Webb.

"He started it," yelled Mr Webb, pointing an accusing finger at his neighbour. The two men began to squabble like two toddlers arguing over a toy. Jim and Dom stared at their fathers in horror, and then turned to look at each other.

"Oh, dear," gasped Jim. "I think we really might have gone too far this time."

"Yes," agreed Dom. "How are we going to put a stop to it before we completely ruin Christmas? The two boys put their head together to think of a solution to their Christmas light dilemma. Then, they sat their dads down and told them what they had decided.

Just twenty minutes later, power was restored and the Christmas lights were dazzling the neighbourhood once more. Only now, they were bigger and better than ever before. The Jones family and the Webb family had joined forces and now they had so many lights flashing, twinkling and glowing that you could barely see the houses beneath. In fact, the whole street was lit up like a lighthouse on overtime. The Battle of the Bulbs was over and Christmas could truly begin.

People from far and wide had crowded into the street to admire the display.

Everyone agreed that the bulbs were even more impressive than the lights on the Town Hall, and soon a reporter from the local newspaper arrived on the scene to take a photograph.

"How did you manage to mount such a marvellous display?" he asked the dads. Mr Jones put an arm around Mr Webb and smiled into the camera.

"Teamwork," answered both dads at once.

"That's right," continued Mr Jones. "We've always got on marvellously and find that working together always works, particularly at this time of year." Behind them Jim and Dom began to giggle. Their mums and Katy joined in.

"Ssshhh," hissed Mr Jones out of the corner of his mouth, just as the photographer pressed the shutter. In the next edition of the paper there was a

picture on the front page. The two dads looked rather embarrassed, while the mums and the children were all howling with laughter!

Stories for Seven to Nine Year Olds

In the front of the car two dark

The Christmas Grump

by Gaby Goldsack

P-109

Peter had really been looking forward to Christmas with his cousin Ben. He just knew it would be heaps better than staying at home on his own with his mum and dad. But that was until they actually arrived at Auntie Lyn and Uncle Jim's house on Christmas Eve. At first everything had seemed the same as normal. Auntie Lyn had given Peter and his parents her usual warm hug. Uncle Jim had pumped Peter's hand enthusiastically as he cracked a terrible joke. Ellie, Peter's three year-old cousin, had given him a shy chocolate-smeared grin. And Danny, Auntie Lyn's soppy labrador, had given Peter a friendly lick on the nose. Then Peter had looked around.

"Where's Ben?" he asked. He was really looking forward to seeing his older cousin because he hadn't seen him for a couple of years.

"Oh, don't ask," laughed Auntie Lyn. "He's probably skulking in his bedroom. He wants to go out to the garage and mess around but I've banned him because I don't want him getting all filthy. You know what teenagers are like."

"No, not really," replied Peter, who didn't know much about teenagers. "Can I go up and say hello?"

"Er, sure," said Uncle Jim. "But don't expect a warm welcome. Ben doesn't say a lot these days."

Peter rushed up the stairs and charged into his cousin's bedroom without knocking. At first he could hardly see a thing because the curtains were drawn and the room was as dark as a cave. Peter squinted his eyes

until he could just make out Ben's gangling
form bent over his computer's keyboard.
His long hair flopped down over his brow
and his face was wrinkled in a furious
frown.

"Yeahwhatnowmum?" grunted
Ben crossly. His eyes didn't
even leave the computer screen.
"Havenyaheardofknocking?"

Peter couldn't really understand
what his cousin was saying but he had
the distinct feeling that he wasn't saying
"Pleased to see you."

"Er, it's me ... Peter," he whispered
shyly. "What did you just say?"

"Oh, yeah," said Ben, looking up and
noticing him for the first time. "I'm busy at
the mo, OK? Catch you later."

Peter was so surprised that he almost
fell backwards as he backed out of the
room and closed the door very quietly

behind him. What had happened to his nice, friendly cousin? He was normally great fun and was always pleased to see Peter. It was as if somebody had kidnapped him and replaced him with a weird grunting monster.

Ben crept slowly down the stairs and went to find his parents. They were in the sitting room admiring Uncle Jim and Auntie Lyn's bushy Christmas tree. Beneath it there were piles and piles of beautifully wrapped presents.

"Cool!" cried Peter, forgetting all about Ben for a second. "Are any of those for me?"

" Of course they are," laughed Auntie Lyn. "Did you say 'hi' to Ben?"

"Sort of," mumbled Peter, hopping from foot to foot and looking rather uncomfortable. "He was kind of busy."

"Busy playing a computer game, I'll

bet," said Uncle Jim, patting Peter on the shoulder.

"The curtains are pulled and it's all dark in there," said Peter. "Is there something wrong with him?"

"No," laughed Auntie Lyn. "He's just a teenage boy. I'll put Ellie to bed. Then I'll get him to say hello properly."

Ten minutes later Auntie Lyn returned with her grumpy-looking son, who was fed up because he'd had to finish his computer game just as it was getting really good. He grunted 'hello' to everyone and then retreated to the corner of the settee. There he remained for the rest of the evening, only venturing out occasionally to grab himself a drink or some nuts or a mince pie. He didn't even say anything when a group of carol singers invaded the drive. He merely slipped off to bed when no one was looking.

Later, while Peter lay in bed waiting for Christmas Day to arrive, he vowed not to let Ben ruin his Christmas.

"If he doesn't want to be friends with me, I don't want to be friends with him," he decided before falling asleep. "In fact, I'm just going to ignore him. I don't think I like teenagers. They're boring!"

The following morning, Peter leapt out of bed and rushed to the window. He clapped his hands with excitement. Overnight it had snowed and now the world was glistening white. Peter rushed into his mum and dad's room.

"Merry Christmas," he cried, bouncing up and down on their bed. "It's been snowing. Get up so we can open our presents, and then we can go outside and make a snowman."

Mum and Dad wiped the sleep from their eyes and yawned.

"What's the time?" Dad asked.

"Time to open our presents," laughed Peter.

"Oh, we can't do that yet," explained Mum. "We promised Auntie Lyn we'd wait until after breakfast. I tell you what. Why don't we get dressed? Then we can go downstairs and start getting things ready."

Peter wasn't happy. At home, they always opened the presents as soon as he woke up. But he did as he was told and got dressed as quickly as he could.

Downstairs Mum put on the kettle and Dad set the breakfast table, while Peter sorted all the presents into piles. Then they waited. At eight o'clock Auntie Lyn and Uncle Jim came downstairs with Ellie.

"I've woken Ben. He should be down shortly," said Uncle Jim. Then Auntie Lyn began to make the breakfast, while Uncle Jim and Peter took the dog for a walk through the snow. When they came back the breakfast was ready but there was still no sign of Ben. Uncle Jim called up the stairs and there was no reply.

"I don't think he's out of bed yet," frowned Uncle Jim. "I'll go and fetch him."

Everyone sat down at the breakfast table for what seemed like ages before

Uncle Jim reappeared with Ben in tow. At this rate they wouldn't have their presents open before midday. Peter was furious. How dare his stupid, grunting cousin ruin Christmas Day! He sniffed loudly, and then jerked his nose in the air before very obviously turning his back on Ben. He was more determined than ever to ignore the annoying teenager, and decided to tell his mum and dad he really didn't want to visit his cousin for Christmas again.

But all thoughts of Ben soon left Peter's head when he began opening his presents. He had lots of brilliant things. There was a model car, a pair of roller blades, some music CDs, the computer game he'd asked for, and, best of all, a book all about classic sports cars. Later, after everyone had finished opening their presents Peter sat on the floor beside the fire to enjoy his new book. He opened the first page and traced his finger over a photograph of a sleek red racing car.

Peter sighed with pleasure. He just

P 119

loved everything about cars. When he was older he wanted to own a car just like the one in the picture. As Peter marvelled over the car's top speed, engine size and general good looks, he didn't notice someone sit down on the chair behind him. But he did notice when that someone let out an admiring grunt. It was Ben. He was looking over Peter's shoulder and reading HIS book. How rude!

Peter whirled round and glared at his cousin.

"Do you mind?" he snapped crossly, and he hunched his shoulders in an effort to block Ben's view.

"Not at all," replied Ben, much to Peter's surprise, and he moved so that he could see into the book once more. "That's not a bad motor," he muttered, pointing at the car Peter was admiring. "But you should see the beauty Dad and I are working on in the garage."

"What?" asked Peter, his ears perking up with interest.

"The beauty Dad and I are working on in the garage," repeated Ben. "It's a real classic. Throaty four-litre, six-cylinder, twin-overhead-cam engine, dual choke carburettors, the lot. Once we finish doing her up, she'll go like a dream."

Peter's mouth gaped wide open. This is the first he'd heard about a mysterious car in the garage.

"Top speed of 140 mph in its day," purred Ben, sounding a bit like a TV presenter. "Would you like to see it? You'll have to use a bit of imagination, mind you. There's still a long way to go before she's finished."

"Yes," cried Peter, jumping to his feet so quickly that his precious book thumped to the ground. He picked up the book and hurried after his cousin. "I'd love to see your car. Please, please, please show me!"

"Okay," said Ben slowly. "But I'd better check with Mum first. She's banned me from the garage for Christmas. She doesn't want me getting all oily or something."

When Auntie Lyn saw how eager Ben
was to show Peter the car she relented
and declared the garage no longer out of
bounds.

"Wicked!" cried Peter, when Ben

swung back the garage door to reveal a
sleek red sports car inside. It was standing
on blocks rather than wheels. Its bonnet

was missing. Its engine had definitely seen better days, and its once shiny chrome radiator grille and bumper were sitting on the workbench rather than on the front. But no one would deny that the car really was a beauty.

Peter followed his cousin around the car and admired it from all angles.

"Can I look inside?" he asked shyly.

"Sure," said Ben, opening the driver's door. "Sit inside. Isn't it great!"

Peter climbed into the car and looked longingly at the steering wheel.

"Go on," said Ben. "Have a play with the steering wheel. It's perfectly safe. You can't go anywhere."

Ben put his hands on the steering wheel, looked in the rear-view mirror, and pretended to drive just like his mum and dad.

"Brrrmmmm, brrrmmmmmm," he

growled softly, imagining he was driving along. Then he quickly stopped when he remembered he was with Ben. After all, he didn't want to remind his cousin that he was just a stupid kid. But he needn't have worried. Ben gave him a big grin and clambered in beside him.

"Brrmmmm, brmmmmm," Ben growled, and soon they were both 'brrmming' and 'beeping' along in a world of their own. They didn't stop until they heard footsteps.

"What are you guys up to?" called Uncle Jim. "It's time for Christmas dinner."

"Come on," said Ben. "We'd better go inside before the oldies get cross."

"Okay," agreed Peter. "Thanks for showing me the car. I'd love to go for a real ride in it one day. That would be just fantastic."

"Well, come back again next

Christmas and we should be able to do just that. With any luck I will have passed my driving test and the car is bound to be ready. There's not much left to do now. Let's go and have dinner, and then afterwards I'll tell you all about our plans."

So, after everyone had finished an enormous, stomach-stretching festive feast, Ben and Peter sat beside the fire and talked about cars. After their food had gone down, they went outside to have a snowball fight and they helped Ellie build her very first snowman. Well, it wasn't actually a snowman; it was more of a snow car!

"Maybe teenagers aren't so bad after all," thought Peter to himself. He had ended up having a brilliant day with Ben because they both liked cars so much.

"Thanks for a great Christmas," he told Ben.

"Yeah, it was OK. I'd have been really

bored without you," Ben grinned. "Brmm, brmmm! See you next year, yeah?"

"Yeah!" smiled Peter.

An Old-Fashioned Christmas

by Gaby Goldsack

P-127

It was Christmas Eve in the year 3000, and Kelly was fast asleep in the space station where she lived. This morning her atomic alarm had failed to go off and now she was late for space school. After stuffing down a vitamin bar, she rushed into her education cubicle and flicked a switch. She tried her best to hide a yawn as Ms Fizz, her holographic teacher, appeared before her.

"You're late," complained Ms Fizz. "That's the third time this week and as a punishment I've decided to set you a special project."

Kelly frowned. Ms Fizz had set her 'special projects' before and they were usually as dull as moon rock.

"Don't look so cross," smiled Ms Fizz. "You might even enjoy this one. As it's Christmas Eve, I thought it might be nice if you could write an essay all about Christmas on Old Earth long ago, in the 21st century. Look, I've even found you an old-fashioned printed book full of wonderful Christmas tales from the past."

There was a zooming noise and a dusty old book appeared from a chute at Kelly's elbow. She was delighted because, although she had lived in space all her life, she loved Old Earth history. She took the book and began flicking through its well-thumbed pages. It was full of strange pictures. There was a jolly old man wearing a red and white suit, eating a spoonful of something round on a plate.

"Who is THAT?" laughed Kelly, pointing at the white-whiskered man. "And what is he eating?"

"That is Father Christmas – the giver of presents," explained Ms Fizz. "And I've no idea what he is eating. Perhaps you could find out."

For the rest of the morning Kelly found it very hard to concentrate on her lessons. While Ms Fizz droned on about intergalactic rocket science, Kelly stared out of a space station porthole and daydreamed about visiting Old Earth. She'd never been there herself, but her grandpa had been born there and never tired of telling her tales about his boyhood.

At noon a siren sounded and Ms Fizz disappeared in a fizzle of space static. Behind her she had left a note on the computer console:

'Don't forget your special project. Five hundred words about Christmas on Old Earth in the 21st century. To be ready by

the next full moon.'

Kelly's home space station was on the far side of the moon. She could see from the window that the moon was half full now, so she hadn't got long to finish the project, and tomorrow was Christmas Day, so she'd be having a few hours break with her family. They'd celebrate Christmas by getting some new things, but all they had to do was go up to a 'replicator' machine and ask for whatever they wanted. It would instantly appear.

Kelly decided to get going on her project straight away. She grabbed the book Ms Fizz had given her and decided to go and see Grandpa. He lived on the other side of the space station so Kelly caught a magnet-shuttle and was there in a couple of minutes. As always, Andrew, Grandpa's personal butler android, was waiting at the door.

"Come in, come in," he cried. "We've been expecting you."

"How?" Kelly asked the robot with a puzzled frown.

"Oh, robots have a way of knowing these things," laughed Andrew.

"And we saw you coming on the closed circuit television," added Grandpa, appearing behind Andrew. "Come on in!"

Kelly was ushered into Grandpa's spacious living room, and quickly told him about the special project Ms Fizz had set her that morning.

"Ooh, what fun!" Grandpa grinned. "I can teach you all about Christmas when I was a boy. Better still I can show you. We can start by making Christmas cards." He immediately started punching words into his computer and soon printed images were spilling out.

"What exactly are Christmas cards?"

asked a puzzled Kelly, as she watched Grandpa pick up a sheet of paper with the giver of presents pictured on the front. He folded it in half and started writing inside.

"They're cards you send people to wish them a Merry Christmas," explained Grandpa. "They have nice pictures on the front so that people can use them as decorations."

"Why bother?" asked Kelly. "Surely it's much easier to send them a text message or virtual greeting?"

"Christmas cards are much nicer," said Grandpa. "You can put a message inside and the picture on the front will make your friends and relatives remember all the good things about Christmas."

"Hmm, that does sound nice," Kelly agreed. "Can I make one for a friend?"

"Of course you can," smiled Grandpa. "And while you do, I'll show you some of my old Christmas digisnaps on the computer."

"And I'll be in the kitchen making some special Christmas treats that your

Grandpa has told me about," added Andrew.

"Why don't you just use the replicator?" asked Kelly with a frown. "All you need to do is tell it what you want and you'll get it instantly."

"But today we're going to do everything the old-fashioned way," Andrew explained. "That means measuring, mixing and cooking properly! Perhaps you'd like to come and help once you've finished making the cards."

"Maybe," said Kelly, who secretly thought that cooking sounded like hard work.

While Kelly made a Christmas card with a jolly Father Christmas on the front, her grandpa brought up some old digisnaps on the computer and told her how he had spent Christmas as a child.

"That's me decorating the Christmas

tree," smiled Grandpa. "Just before Christmas we'd go out and buy the biggest, bushiest Christmas tree we could find. Then we'd take it home and decorate it with tinsel, fancy balls and bright sparkly lights."

"What for?" asked Kelly, thinking how strange such a thing would look in her space-age home.

"It made the house look festive and jolly," explained Grandpa. "Then, on Christmas Eve, we'd hang our stockings on the end of our beds and go to sleep early. While we were asleep Father Christmas would come and leave us lots of lovely gifts. We always got lots of wonderful surprises. One year I even got a bicycle. Look, there I am in the photo, ripping off all the wrapping paper."

"That does look fun," said Kelly, thinking how much nicer it sounded than

simply going to the replicator on Christmas morning.

"Here we are having our Christmas dinner," said Grandpa, as up popped a picture of a laughing family sat around a laden table. It all looked so good that Kelly's mouth began to water.

"After we opened all the presents, friends and relatives came round and we'd have a special Christmas meal."

"Hey, what's that you're pulling in that picture? And why have you all got silly hats on your head?" laughed Kelly.

"That's a cracker I'm pulling with my little sister. When you pulled them apart they went CRACK and out fell a gift, a silly joke and, best of all, a paper hat to wear while you ate dinner. It all just helped to make Christmas Day feel special."

Kelly thought it all sounded very bizarre but kind of fun as well. Although she wasn't at all sure she'd be caught dead in a silly paper hat, even on Christmas Day.

"Anyone for a quick stir? I'm making Christmas cake," announced Andrew, appearing with a bowl of gooey mixture in his hand.

"Ah, this is another Old Earth Christmas tradition," said Grandpa, leading Kelly into the kitchen. "You stir the Christmas cake mixture and make a wish. Go on, give it a go but don't tell us your wish."

Kelly stirred the cake and closed her eyes. She thought for a moment then wished as hard as she could.

When they had all made their wish Kelly looked around the kitchen and sniffed with pleasure. It smelt warm, spicy and delicious. On the table was a round pudding, which glistened with fruit.

"I've seen that in a picture!" Kelly exclaimed.

"That's a Christmas pudding," explained Grandpa.

"Can I have some now?" Kelly asked.

"No," laughed Andrew. "You can eat some at the special Old Earth Christmas dinner we are throwing tomorrow. We're even going to have crackers and a beautiful Christmas tree."

"And who knows, Father Christmas might even bring you a surprise or two," added Grandpa.

Kelly shook her head in wonder. "An old-fashioned Christmas is exactly what I wished for when I stirred the Christmas cake. However did you guess?" she asked.

"Oh, robots have a way of knowing these things," said Andrew.

"And Ms Fizz told me all about your 'special project'," laughed Grandpa. "I thought it would be a good way of helping you to learn about Christmas on Old Earth. I've invited the whole family, and Ms Fizz, too. Come on, there's a lot to do between now and tomorrow…and using the replicator is cheating!"

Kelly clapped her hands with excitement. She knew it would be hard work, making decorations, helping Andrew to bake treats, and choosing presents to wrap. But she also knew it was going to be the best Christmas ever!

The Christmas Cook-Off

by Gaby Goldsack

As soon as Chrissy saw the poster for the competition, she just knew that Granny Green had to enter.

Granny Green made the best cakes ever, and her Christmas cake was simply scrumptious. Chrissy picked up an entry form and rushed over to Granny Green's house. Today was the 14 December, so there wasn't a moment to lose.

As always, Granny Green's house smelt delicious. Chrissy sniffed the air. The scent was a mixture of baking, furniture polish, and… What was that? Oh, yes, there was just a hint of pine needles from the small Christmas tree in the hall.

"Hi," called Chrissy, as she charged into the warm, cosy kitchen.

"Hello," smiled Granny Green. She gave Chrissy a warm, floury hug, then bent down to pull something out of the oven. "I've made you some of those mince pies you love so much."

"Can I have one now?" asked Chrissy greedily.

"No," laughed Granny Green, batting away Chrissy's hovering hand. "They're far too hot. You'll have to wait until they've cooled down."

"Well, while I wait, take a look at this." Chrissy pulled the now crumpled form out of her pocket.

"Now, let me see," said Granny Green, carefully placing her spectacles on the end of her nose. She held the piece of paper at arm's length and began to read silently to herself.

Chrissy waited eagerly for her to say something. After what seemed like forever, Granny Green put the form down and began to chuckle. Chrissy frowned with confusion.

"What are you laughing at?" she demanded crossly. "Your Christmas cakes are fabulous and I've always wanted to have a Christmas holiday in the snow."

Granny Green gave Chrissy a hug.

"Bless you," she smiled. "My Christmas cake might be good but I don't think it's world-beating. Anyone who is anyone will enter. There will be master chefs from all over the world. There's no way your silver-haired granny stands any chance of making it through to the final, let alone winning."

"But Dad always says you make the best Christmas cake in the world," declared Chrissy. "And you always win Best in Show at the Christmas Fair."

"I'm not saying that my Christmas cake isn't good," smiled Granny Green. "But I'm not at all sure it's great."

"Well I am," cried Chrissy. "Please enter. Pretty please!"

Granny Green looked at Chrissy's eager face and began to weaken.

"Hmm," she said slowly. "I don't suppose it would hurt to send my entry in."

"Hooray," cried Chrissy. "Now we haven't got much time, so you'd better getting writing. Then I'll post it straight away. Come on, hurry!"

While Granny Green sat down to fill in her entry form, Chrissy found a stamp and an envelope.

"It says here that anyone who qualifies for the 'cook off' can take an assistant along. Do you know of anyone who might want to give me a hand?" Granny smiled.

"Me, me, me," cried Chrissy, jumping from one foot to the other with excitement. "I'm great at helping. Remember how I

helped you weigh out all the ingredients for Mum's birthday cake? I'm a great washer-upper, too!"

"Oh, that's right," smiled Granny Green. "I'll put you down then, shall I?"

"Yes please," cried Chrissy, breathless with excitement.

"I'll do a deal with you. I'll let you help me make my cake, and if we win you can teach me how to snowboard!" laughed Granny Green.

"Cool!" grinned Chrissy.

Chrissy was at Granny Green's house two days later when the telephone rang.

Granny Green picked it up and began to nod her head with excitement. She said nothing for a while, and then said a quiet 'thank you' before putting the phone down. She turned to Chrissy with a shocked look on her face.

"What is it?" gasped Chrissy. "Has something bad happened?"

"No," said Granny Green slowly. "Something wonderful has happened. Dig out your best clothes. We're going to be on TV. We're through to the final!"

Chrissy jumped up and hugged her gran.

"I knew you'd get through," she laughed.

Just a few days later, Chrissy and Granny Green were lined up beside the rest of the finalists at the big cook-off. Chrissy looked around nervously. They were surrounded by men and women dressed in pristine chef's hats and baggy checked trousers. She even recognized one or two of them from the television. The man next to them had a long thin moustache and talked in a loud voice.

"Of course, I've cooked cakes for kings and queens," he told anyone who would listen.

"The Sultan always says my cake is simply divine," interrupted a man with an even louder voice and the tallest chef's hat Chrissy had ever seen.

As the competition was about to begin, everyone around them began setting up screens.

"What are they doing?" Chrissy asked Granny Green.

"I don't think they want us to know their secret ingredients," replied Granny Green, nervously flicking an invisible speck off her flowery apron. "Do you think I've dressed all wrong?"

"No," said Chrissy firmly. "You look perfect. And we don't need to steal anyone's secret ingredients. Your cake is bound to be better than all the rest put together." But inside Chrissy wasn't feeling quite so certain. She hadn't expected the competition to be as fierce or professional. The best chefs from all over the world were there. Her tummy began to feel all tingly and nervous. Her fingers and thumbs began to feel clumsy. She hoped she wouldn't let Granny Green down. Perhaps it would have been better if she'd got her mum to be Granny's assistant. But before she could suggest it, the bell rang and the great 'cook-off' began.

For the next thirty minutes, Chrissy had no time to be nervous as she helped her gran measure and mix all the ingredients lovingly together. When the

cake finally went into the oven, Chrissy
and Granny Green slumped into their seats
with exhaustion. Their faces were shiny
and red and they were both covered from
head to foot in a dusting of flour. Chrissy
looked around. Everyone else looked calm
and confident, with barely a hair out of
place.

While the cake baked, Granny Green and Chrissy sat in front of the oven holding hands. They didn't dare move. Meanwhile, all the other chefs (who all seemed to know one another) swanned around boasting about who they had cooked for and what television programmes they had made. When one lady mentioned that her Christmas cake was sold in the most exclusive stores around the world, Chrissy and Granny looked at each other and groaned.

"I'm sorry, but I don't think we'll be having a white Christmas," said Granny Green sadly.

"Never mind," replied Chrissy, forgetting all about being encouraging. "Christmas will be great anyway, and your Christmas cake will always be a winner in my eyes."

Just then, the timer rang and Granny

Green rushed to the oven. Chrissy held her breath as her gran pulled the cake out of the oven.

"Let it be good," she prayed silently. Then, as she caught sight of the cake she let out a sigh. It looked perfect and it smelt absolutely gorgeous. She looked around proudly, and then gulped. All the other cakes looked great as well.

Once the cakes had cooled, they were lined up before three stern-looking judges, who held forks in their hands. One by one, they made their way down the line.

"Great. Not bad. Too dry. Too rich. Fantastic. Marvellous," they commented as they munched their way through the cakes. Granny Green's cake was the last in the line. As the judges stood before it, prodding, poking and sniffing, Chrissy and Granny Green bit their lips. The first judge took a forkful and began to chew it around. Then he smiled and nodded with approval. The second judge took a taste and sighed with pleasure. The third swirled some around his chubby cheeks. "Simply scrumptious," he declared. The three judges glanced at one another and nodded.

"I think we have a winner. And it's Granny Green," cried the chubby-cheeked judge.

As the audience erupted with applause, Granny Green and Chrissy hugged each other with joy. The other competitors looked very fed-up because they had been beaten by a silver-haired granny and her tiny assistant.

"Come on, you two," cried the judges. "Come and receive your prize."

"Thank you, thank you," whispered Granny Green shyly as she was stood in front of the television audience. Chrissy wasn't feeling half as shy, and she looked into the camera and grinned. Now everyone in the world knew just how special her gran was, and on top of that the whole family was going on a wonderful Christmas holiday in the snow.

"Would you mind telling us all what makes your cake quite so spectacular?" asked the chief judge. "Or is it a secret ingredient?"

The other chefs stopped their huffing and puffing and listened in eagerly. They all wanted to know the secret.

"I don't mind at all," smiled Granny Green, turning to smile at Chrissy. "I don't have a secret ingredient, but I do have a special one. Each and every one of my cakes is made with a sprinkle of love, and I always add an extra dash to my Christmas cakes."

There was a moment of silence and then the audience began to clap and stamp their feet. The other chefs looked at each other and, one by one, they began to smile and clap.

Granny Green winked at Chrissy.

"Are you ready to teach your granny to snowboard?" she asked, as she was handed the tickets for a trip to Winter Wonderland.

"You mean my celebrity granny!" replied Chrissy. "Let's go!"

The Christmas Jumper

by Kath Jewitt

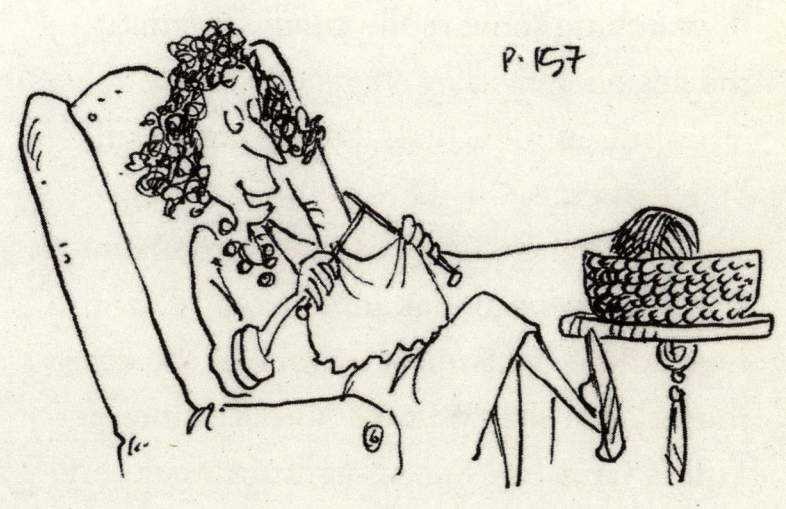

P. 157

You might think that a lively fun-loving boy such as Jack would feel fed up when he was taken to visit his great auntie for a day during the Christmas holidays. After all, he could have been playing with his friends at home, or watching some really good Christmas movies on TV.

But, in fact, Jack didn't mind at all. Why? Because, as Dad pointed out in the car on the way, "There's always Aunt Polly's present to look forward to!" When Dad said it, he winked at Jack in the car mirror, and Jack grinned. Great Aunt Polly's Christmas presents were legendary. Last year she had knitted the whole family matching pink and purple bobble hats.

"I wonder what it'll be this year?" Jack giggled, as the car finally turned into Aunt Polly's drive. "Scarves to match our hats, perhaps? Or maybe fluffy socks!"

"Hush!" warned Mum, waving at Aunt Polly, who was waiting for them on the doorstep. "Your aunt might be old, but she's not deaf. Whatever you do, be polite. And DON'T laugh – even if it's pink and purple underpants!"

A few hours later, Jack and his parents emerged from Great Aunt Polly's house, wearing brand new Christmas jumpers. Jack's really was quite something! It was luminous orange, and had a huge reindeer on the front, with a fluffy red pompom nose. Great Aunt Polly had even knitted a matching orange hat with reindeer antlers and a bell on the top.

"Try it on for size," she had said,

popping the hat on Jack's head, just before they left. "I made a large one, so it will fit you for longer."

"Perhaps I could borrow your hat," suggested Dad, as they finally drove off, "when my pink and purple one is in the wash, of course!"

Jack giggled as he took off his jumper.

"Maybe we could use my hat as a Christmas decoration," he suggested, jingling the bell enthusiastically.

"Don't be silly," said Mum, trying to sound cross. "It's a very... original... present!" But Jack could tell she didn't really mean it. The twitching at the corners of her mouth gave her away.

Jack gazed out of the window at the dark sky, and noticed soft flakes of snow beginning to fall. Soon, he closed his eyes and fell asleep. When he awoke, the snow was falling so heavily that it was hard to see out of the window. It was very cold in the car, too. Jack decided to put on Great Aunt Polly's hat and jumper again.

"I never thought I'd actually CHOOSE to wear these," he thought, pulling the hat down over his ears. "Thank goodness no one from school can see me! I'd be a laughing stock ..."

Dad interrupted his train of thought.

"I think we need to find somewhere to stop," he announced, sounding worried. "The car heater has packed up. I think there might be something wrong with the engine. Even if it keeps going, we're going to freeze at this rate."

Mum pointed at a snow-covered sign.

"Look," she said. "There's a motorway service station in a few miles. We can pull in there and check out the car. If we have to, we can stay the night at the motel."

But the weather had other plans for

them. By the time they had driven just a few miles further, the snow was falling so heavily that it was almost impossible to see ahead. The already slow traffic began to crawl along. Finally it came to a stop.

Jack shivered and rubbed his hands together.

"I wish Aunt Polly had made matching gloves!" he said, trying to smile. "What do we do now?"

"We stay here until the blizzard stops," said Mum firmly. "It would be dangerous to wander about in this weather. We could easily get lost."

"But I'm freezing!" cried Jack. "How long will we be stuck here?"

"Not long," said Dad, in his 'everything will be fine' voice. "Someone will be along to rescue us soon."

Mum nodded. "Let's huddle together in the back to keep warm," she suggested.

"We can eat the chocolate log cake Aunt Polly made for us. And if you don't fancy it, we can burn it to keep warm."

"Bad joke!" groaned Jack. But it did make him feel better, all the same.

"Hey Mum!" he said. "I've got one for you. Where does Santa stay on his holidays? A ho...ho...hotel!"

Half an hour, and far too many jokes later, a police light began to flash outside in the snow.

"Here's help at last," said Mum, straining to see through the snow-covered window. "They must have come to rescue us!"

"Hurray!" cheered Jack, whose fingers were beginning to go numb by now. "But what about our car?"

"It will be fine here," said Dad. "We can come and fetch it when the road is open again."

The police had made arrangements for all the stranded travellers to take shelter in a nearby village hall. So it wasn't long before Jack and his family were sitting in the warm again, with blankets round their shoulders, drinking hot soup from a mug.

Mum put her arm around Jack's shoulder and gave him a squeeze.

"Warmed up yet?" she asked.

Jack nodded. "Can we go home soon?" he asked. Mum shook her head.

"We may have to stay for the night," she explained. "I just heard a policeman say the cars on the roadside are buried under the snow now."

"Great," frowned Jack grumpily. "What am I going to do all night? There's no telly, no games, no books ... This day can't get any worse!"

But Jack was wrong. It could get worse, and it did. At that very moment, another group of stranded travellers came in through the door. At first Jack didn't think anything of it. Then he distinctly heard the words 'weird' and 'reindeer' and a burst of wild laughter. Jack looked up. In the doorway, wrapped in blankets from head to toe, were three kids, and they were all staring in his direction. Of course! Jack had forgotten he was still wearing Great Aunt Polly's ludicrous reindeer hat and jumper! To make matters worse, he recognized one boy. He was one of the kids in a football team that Jack's team sometimes played.

Jack blushed crimson. How embarrassing could you get? He'd been caught wearing a luminous orange jumper and a reindeer hat by a rival footballer. He would NEVER live this down at the next match. It would be awful.

Jack snatched off the offending hat and stuffed it in his pocket, thinking fast.

"He probably hasn't recognized me yet," he decided. "If I can just stay out of his way until we go, I might get away with it. But I've got to ditch this stupid jumper and hat ..."

Jack waited until the boy and his friends were queueing for soup, then quickly slipped the hat and jumper under some blankets in the corner of the room. Just as he was congratulating himself on a job well done, an old lady tapped him on the shoulder.

"I think you've lost your lovely hat and jumper, dear!" she smiled, returning the offending items with a smile. "I found them in the blanket pile just now. We all knew at once they belonged to you. We spotted you wearing them when we came in! Were they a Christmas present? Quite a challenging design to knit, you know ..."

Out of the corner of his eye, Jack caught sight of someone waving. It was the football kid, and he had a big cheesy grin on his face.

"I'm sorry," mumbled Jack, feeling himself go red. "I have to go!"

Filled with shame, he grabbed his knitted nightmares and rushed off to the cloakroom to hide. The football kid had definitely recognized him. He was certain of that. The boy was bound to blab to everyone in his team, and then Jack's own players would find out and find the story just as funny. There would be no escaping the teasing.

Just then, the cloakroom door swung open, and in walked the football kid, still tightly wrapped in his blanket.

"Hello," he grinned cheekily. "Aren't you one of the boys I've played at football?" Jack nodded miserably.

"My name's Ben," said the football kid, still grinning from ear to ear. "What's happened to your reindeer hat and jumper?"

Jack swallowed hard. "What do you mean?" he asked. "I don't ..."

Suddenly, the cloakroom door opened again, and the old lady popped her head round.

"Oh hello, Ben!" she smiled. "I see you've met the young man who owns the lovely reindeer hat and jumper. Aren't they super? Well, I expect I'll see you two boys later." And with that, she disappeared.

"Do you two know each other?" asked Jack, feeling completely confused. Ben nodded, and started to laugh.

"That," he said, "is my granny. And THIS ..." he continued, taking off his blanket "... is what she gave me for Christmas! What do you think?"

For a moment, Jack stared in disbelief. Ben was wearing a hideous lime green jumper with a huge Christmas pudding on the front. There were even Christmas bells sewn on the top of the pudding! Even by the standards of Jack's own jumper collection, Ben's knitted nightmare had to be one of the most hideous ever created.

"Gran knits a special Christmas jumper for me and my cousins every year! We call them our geek gear."

"And I thought I was the only uncool kid around here!" laughed Jack.

Ben grinned.

"I won't tell if you don't tell," he said. "Shall we shake on it?"

"OK! Hold on a moment," grinned Jack and he jammed his reindeer hat, with its

own bell, back on his head. "Are you ready? Let's shake!"

The sound of Christmas bells tinkled from the cloakroom, mixed in with giggles from two laughing boys!

Crazy but Cool

by Moira Butterfield

Jon knew his friend Rob had had a
crazy idea, because he could see
that Rob was almost bouncing with
excitement when he rang Jon's front door
bell about a month before Christmas. Rob
was always coming up with daft plans,
each one more complicated than the last,
usually involving Jon and all with one aim
– to make some money! None of Rob's
schemes had worked so far, but it didn't
stop him trying. This time he seemed really
certain of success.

"I've had the most brilliant idea
ever," he announced grandly. Jon sighed,
sat down and waited to hear about the
brainwave, knowing he wasn't going to
get out of helping. He'd tried before and

there just wasn't any point. Rob was like a whirlwind when he got started on any new plan, and resistance was useless. Anyway, his moneymaking schemes were usually quite fun, if occasionally disastrous. There was the time they'd offered to look after all the pets in the neighbourhood during the summer holidays, and then had to chase after two escaping guinea pigs and a budgie. Then there was the time they'd cooked lots of sweets to sell, but got salt mixed up with the sugar and had to give all the money back when their customers tried out the sweets, felt sick and complained. But Jon had to admit that this time, Rob's idea sounded pretty good.

"There's this new shop in town," Rob explained. "It's a printing shop."

Rob handed Jon a leaflet he'd picked up from the new store, announcing a Christmas card printing offer:

Be creative this year. Give us your own picture or photo and we will make it into a unique printed Christmas card.

Then the leaflet had a list of prices.

"That looks expensive!" Jon pointed out.

"No, it's not. If we do a really great photo we can sell the cards and make a profit," Rob explained.

"Well…," Jon hesitated.

"Come on! You've seen those millionaire businessmen on TV, haven't you? They sell stuff and end up making enough money to buy seventeen houses," Rob cried.

"We'd never sell that many Christmas cards," Jon pointed out.

"I know, but it'd be a start. Look, I've brought all my pocket money over," Rob said, turning out his pockets. "If you add yours we'll have enough."

Jon wandered to himself why Rob's schemes always turned out to need his pocket money. Still, this really did seem like a good way to make some extra cash and then he'd be able to buy some special Christmas presents for his family.

"What kind of Christmas card do you think we should do?" he asked, thinking perhaps of a drawing of a Christmas tree or a jolly Santa.

"I've thought of that," Rob grinned. "I'll borrow my sister's digital camera. She said I could if I was careful. Then we'll take a fantastic wildlife photo!"

"Eh?" Jon asked incredulously.

"You've seen those wildlife programmes on TV, haven't you?" Rob asked. Jon was beginning to think Rob was watching too much TV.

"I saw one the other day with tigers rolling in snow. That'd make a great

Christmas card shot. There was one with baby polar bears, too. They were cute. Everyone loves pictures of cute animals," Rob declared.

"So, let's get this straight," Jon spoke extra-slowly and clearly to his plainly crazy friend. "You want us to take photos of tigers and baby polar bears in the snow. Now, forgive me if I'm wrong, but I haven't recently noticed either of those animals locally, and there isn't any snow."

"Hmm. The snow might be a problem, but not the wildlife. There are loads of birds and things running around outside. We'll get our shot and sell masses of cards," Rob explained, and Jon had to agree. It sounded foolproof!

The next day, bright and early, Rob and Jon took the digital camera outside. Sadly there was no snow, but Rob had thought of that. He had brought along one

of his mum's white bedsheets and a pair of
toy reindeer antlers that his sister had worn
at a Christmas party last year.

"OK. Now we need your cat," he
declared.

"You mean Tiddles?" Jon asked,
confused.

"Yup. Tiddles will become a cute-
looking reindeer-cat with these on his head,
as he pads over the snow," Rob explained.

"Bedsheet," Jon corrected him.

"Whatever. It's going to be the cutest
looking Christmas card ever," Rob insisted.

But unfortunately Tiddles was not
keen on having a pair of reindeer antlers
anywhere near him. When Jon called him
over he took one suspicious look at the
boys, turned tail and disappeared into the
bushes, leaving a trail of muddy pawprints
across the bedsheet as he fled.

"Oh well. No-one ever said wildlife

photography was easy," Rob muttered. "On to Plan B. Go and get some biscuits, will you, Jon?"

Jon knew better than to argue with the genius Christmas card creator and besides, he fancied a biscuit himself, so he went indoors and returned with a couple of yummy chocolate biscuits, or rather one-and-a-half biscuits because he'd tried one on the way.

Rob crumbled the biscuits over the bedsheet and then the two friends hid behind a garden chair with the camera pointing at the scene.

"Yes!" Rob whispered triumphantly as birds began to appear, fluttering down onto the sheet to peck at the crumbs.

"They're not as cuddly as baby polar bears but they're not bad," he grinned. He aimed the camera and pressed the button to take a photo, but nothing happened.

"Oh no! The camera battery's flat," he said loudly, and all the birds flew away, leaving a mess of chocolate and crumbs behind them. The sheet was looking less and less like snow and more like a piece of dirty laundry. The boys trooped indoors, feeling a bit deflated.

But there was one thing you could always say about Rob. He never gave up.

The next day he was back at Jon's door, this time with his arms full. Not only did he have the digital camera with new batteries inside, but he had a dead-looking plant and a bag of flour.

"It's going to be perfect!" he cried. "This is my neighbour's old Christmas tree from last year. It's really good, isn't it?"

"Er…" Jon said, not liking to point out that it was all brown and dried-up.

"Great! Have you any more of those biscuits?" Rob asked, striding confidently through to the back door. Outside he stood the worn-out Christmas tree on the path. Then he poured flour around it and dusted some onto the tree branches. Jon had to admit it did look quite like snow, though he wasn't sure what his mum was going to say when she saw a pile of flour in the back garden.

Rob busied himself scattering crumbs

around the tree.

"The birds will come down and we'll get a shot of them by the tree," he explained.

"Hold on a minute," grinned Jon. He popped indoors, found a couple of old dishclothes and stuffed them with biscuit and a few raisins. Then he tied them on to to the tree branches.

"What a feast for the birds," Rob declared. "They won't resist coming down, and we'll be here to photograph them. Nothing can go wrong!"

Once again they settled down quietly to wait for their photo opportunity and, sure enough, the birds soon arrived. They seemed to love the treats the boys had put out and they obligingly posed on the tree branches and wandered around in the flour while Rob snapped loads of photos.

Eventually Tiddles turned up. He

scared away the birds and got flour all over his nose and paws, but even that made for a cute photo, and soon the boys reckoned they had plenty to choose from. They rushed indoors and downloaded the photos onto Jon's dad's computer.

"Wow! They don't look bad," Jon cried excitedly.

"Never in doubt," Rob grinned.

They spent the rest of the afternoon choosing the very best photo.

"I'll get my dad to put it on to a disk and we can take in to the shop tomorrow," Jon suggested, but later he decided to try to put the photo on a disk himself. He really wanted to keep the card project a secret from his parents so he could surprise them with extra-expensive Christmas presents. He'd seen his dad download stuff before, and he reckoned he knew how. Rob wasn't the only one with money-making skills!

The boys arrived excitedly at the printing shop the next day. They filled in an order form and handed over their money and their photo on a computer disk. The printer promised to get the cards ready by the end of the week.

Rob and Jon had fun planning how they would spend the money once they had sold the cards for a profit.

"I'm going to buy some great presents for everyone, as a big surprise. Then I'm going to get a new box of chocolate biscuits," Jon said.

"I'd like to buy new football boots," Rob replied, and he was describing them when Jon's mum called him to the phone. It was the printer.

"Are you sure this picture is what you want?" the man asked.

"Yes, it is," Jon replied. He was annoyed that the printer was being rude, presumably about their tree and the flour.

"It's meant to be snow," Jon explained.

"Well, alright, if you say so," the printer replied.

"Yes I do," Jon whispered, and put down the phone before his mum could hear any more.

Finally the day arrived when the cards were ready, and the boys rushed to the printing shop as soon as they could.

"Oh, hello," the printer greeted them. "Here is your box of cards, as ordered."

The boys opened the box triumphantly and took out a packet of cards.

""W..w..what?" Rob spluttered. "There's nothing on the front!"

"Yes there is. It says 'Happy Christmas'," the printer replied, pointing to some words at the top of an otherwise blank white card.

"Where is our photo?" Jon demanded, but he was already getting a sinking feeling that this was his fault.

"That is your photo. It's all there was on the disk. I rang you about it, remember?" the printer replied, folding his arms. "You said it was meant to represent snow."

"I don't understand," Rob whispered, his face a picture of shock.

Happy Christmas

"I must have done something wrong on the computer…" Jon muttered, feeling very embarrassed. There was a stunned silence as Jon thought about the wasted time, pocket money and chocolate biscuits, and Rob thought about the new football boots he wouldn't be getting.

Then a voice boomed out behind them.

"Oh, what genius!"

A smartly-dressed man stood in the shop, peering over their shoulders at the blank cards.

"The white emptiness represents snow, you say. What brilliant imaginations you boys have. I'll buy all your cards. My arty friends will love them," he announced. He produced a roll of banknotes from his pocket and handed them over!

"Does your work have a title? Every great work of art has a title," he asked.

Jon thought for a moment, then got inspiration when he looked over at his mad friend Rob.

"I think we'll call it 'crazy but cool'," he grinned. "Just like us!"